Bartending for

Beginners

A Beginner's Guide to the Basics of Bartending Which Will Quickly Teach You to Mix Cocktails and Perform Bar Tricks Like a Pro (Recipes, Terminology, Techniques and More)

By Bruno Gordon

Contents

Thank you for buying this book and I hope that you will find it useful. If you will want to share your thoughts on this book, you can do so by leaving a review on the Amazon page, it helps me out a lot.

INTRODUCTION

" So a man strolls into a bar and asks the bartender ..." How many jokes have you heard begin that way. The bartender is the primary focus of every commercial bar. Forget about the waitresses. Definitely, they bring the beverages. However, the bartender needs to make them. Forget about the fry cooks dishing out oily french fries. It's the bartender who has actually made you yearn for them.

Bartenders have actually delighted in a long and storied history. They are the psychiatrists that you do not need to have an appointment for. They are the ones you hear all the greatest jokes from. They are the ones who reveal you the neatest bar tricks to impress your buddies. The bartender, for some individuals, is the very best buddy they never ever had.

Tending to bars is more than simply pouring a cold draught beer or blending a mean screwdriver. With all the brand-new cocktail mixes out nowadays, bartenders should be up on all the brand-new terms, not to mention having the capability to mix up an Alabama Slammer without searching in the recipe handbook.

Bartending schools are appearing all over the nation. Enticed by the temptation of money tips for serving the drunken public, bartending has actually risen to an art form. When the film "Cocktail" appeared, bartenders looked for the capability to twirl bottles and toss them up in the air as the bottle pours an ideal shot before it lands gently in their hand. Few can argue this is a thing the ordinary Joe can not accomplish.

Whether you aspire to the "Cocktail" popularity made popular by Tom Cruise, or if you simply wish to have an excellent house bar, this book is going to look into all elements of bartending.

I'll inform you how to have a well-stocked house bar and a well-stocked commercial bar. I'll describe a few of the terms related to partaking of liquors and supply you with a number of the most prominent recipes asked for on Spring Break or in your local club.

Much better than that, I'll offer you some quite remarkable bar tricks you can utilize!

So, let's begin!

Chapter 1: The Professional Bartender

A bartender is somebody who serves drinks behind a licensed bar to paying patrons. A bartender can additionally be referred to as a barkeep or a barmaid. Bartenders are located in bars, pubs, taverns, clubs and other such locations.

The bartender blends and serves beverages, and most of the beverages a bartender is making consist of alcohol, like beer, wine, liquor, coolers and mixed drinks. They likewise serve water, juice, pop and other non-alcoholic drinks for individuals who do not want to consume alcohol like an appointed driver or a non-drinker.

In addition to creating and serving beverages, the bartender is likewise responsible for taking payment for beverages (either from consumers, waiters or waitresses), maintaining the alcohol supplies and glasses stocked, maintaining the bar area tidy, preserving plenty of ice and garnishes on hand and serving food to patrons sitting at the bar, in case the bar provides food for sale.

Typically, the bartender is expected to dress properly to contribute to the environment of the bar. In some facilities, the bartender may take part in flair bartending, which adds to the entertainment in the bar.

Bartenders are counted on to be equipped to mix numerous kinds of drinks to satisfy any paying customer in a fast, precise and non-wasteful style. In some facilities, like a hectic club, the bartender is just expected to serve the customer a beverage and absolutely nothing else. In a tinier location such as a pub, however, the bartender may be counted on to be an excellent listener, and permit the customers to have a shoulder to weep on.

All bartenders must be friendly, nevertheless, and delight in having contact and interaction with individuals. Great bartenders have a method of drawing in regular customers. Great bartenders like this are going to remember the preferred beverage of frequent customers; have beverage recommendations handy or recommendations for other bars, in addition to numerous other informal tasks.

In a lot of countries , tipping is assumed of the customer, and this is how the bartender gets most of his earnings, as many bartenders are paid minimum wage.

In some locations, minors are allowed in bars, and it is the bartender's duty to look for identification prior to offering them alcohol.

If this seems like a great deal of work, with very little reward, look on the bright side. You are operating at a facility that serves gallons of alcohol every day, and you supervise it. The task of a bartender is management, customer care, and so much more! Even a bartending job appears great on a resume when you demonstrate it in the correct way!

Before you begin to tend bars-- whether it's as a job or in your own house, an excellent grasp of terms could be a terrific resource.

Chapter 2: Terminology

A great deal of the terms and expressions listed below are common throughout the industry. A great professional bartender is going to understand his/her profession completely. If you're simply tending bars in your home, you're sure to make an impression on individuals with your large understanding.

Here are a few of the more typical terms utilized in bartending.

Box

Pour the beverage into and out of a shaker, typically just once. This provides the drink with fast blending without shaking.

Call Drink

Alcohol and mixer, of which the alcohol is a name brand (ie. Tanqueray and Tonic, Bacardi and Coke, and so on.).

Chaser

A chaser is a mixer that is taken in right away after a straight shot of alcohol to produce a different taste.

Cocktail

This could be any of different alcoholic beverages consisting generally of brandy, scotch, vodka, or gin mixed with fruit juices or other alcohols and typically served cooled.

Collins

A beverage comparable to a sour which is served in a high glass with soda or seltzer water.

Cooler

A drink being composed of ginger ale, soda, and a fresh spiral or twist of citrus fruit skin and offered in a Collins or highball glass.

Crusta

A sour-type beverage served in a glass that is entirely lined with an orange or lemon peel cut in a constant strip.

Cup

A punch-type beverage that is comprised in quantities of cups or glasses in preference to a punch bowl.

Daisy

A large-scale beverage of the sour kind, typically created with rum or gin. It is offered over crushed ice with a straw and sweetened with a fruit syrup.

Lace

Generally applies to the final ingredient in a recipe which is poured on top of the beverage.

Eggnog

A standard vacation beverage consisting of a mix of eggs beaten with cream or milk, sugar, and an alcohol like rum, brandy, or bourbon.

Fix

A sour-type beverage comparable to the daisy created with crushed ice in a big goblet.

Fizz

An effervescent drink-- one which is carbonated and gives off little bubbles.

Flip

A cooled, velvety beverage made from eggs, sugar, and a wine or spirit. Brandy and sherry flips are 2 of the better-known types of flips.

Frappe

This is a partly frozen, frequently fruity beverage. It is typically a mix of ingredients offered over a pile of crushed ice.

Grog

A rum-based drink with water, fruit juice, and sugar typically served in a big mug.

Highball

Any spirit offered with ice and soda in a medium to high glass (a highball glass).

Julep

A beverage composed of bourbon, mint, sugar, and smashed ice.

Lowball

A short beverage composed of spirits served with ice, water, or soda in a little glass.

Mist

An alcohol served over a glass full of smashed ice-- frequently as is the case with an after-dinner drink.

Mulls

A sweetened and spiced heated alcohol, wine, or beer offered as a hot punch.

Neat

The drinking of a spirit as a direct, unaccompanied shot.

Nip

A quarter of a bottle.

Nightcap

Wine or alcohol typically drunk right before bedtime.

On The Rocks

A beverage served over ice.

Pick-Me-Up

A drink created to ease the impacts of overindulgence in alcohol.

Punch

A party-size drink being composed of fruit, fruit juices, flavorings and sweeteners, sodas, and a wine or alcohol base.

Rickey

A beverage composed of an alcohol, generally gin, a half lime and soda. It is, in some cases, sweetened and typically served with ice.

Shooter

A straight shot of alcohol taken neat.

Sling

A beverage created with either brandy, scotch, or gin together with lemon juice, sugar, and soda water. It is offered both cold and hot.

Sour

A short drink comprising of alcohol, lemon or lime juice and sugar.

Toddy

A sweetened beverage of alcohol and hot water, frequently with seasonings.

Tot

A tiny amount of alcohol.

Virgin

A non-alcoholic beverage.

Well Drink

An alcohol and mixer of which neither are defined brand names (ie. Gin and tonic, rum and coke).

So we have the terms down. Now let's take a look at what a well-stocked bar appears like.

Chapter 3: Stocking Your Bar

Stocking a commercial bar and stocking a house bar are most likely going to be 2 totally separate things unless you want to devote countless dollars on your house bar. In case you are, by all means, follow the list word for word! The liquor store will adore you! Initially, we'll take a look at the common commercial bar stock list.

Stocking a Commercial Bar

You'll wish to make certain you have all the required liquors, mixers, and garnishes to make your patrons pleased. If somebody orders a slippery nipple and you do not have any butterscotch schnapps, you most likely will not have a return customer. Even though it certainly depends upon how desperately they desire that shot!

When it pertains to liquors, here is a list of basics:

Gin

Vodka

Rum (Light and Dark)

Whiskey

Bourbon

Scotch

Rye/Canadian

Irish Cream

Wine

White (Dry)

Red (Dry)

Champagne Vermouth (Dry/Sweet).

Tequila

Brandy/Cognac

Beer

Fruits are essential as garnishes, having lots of the appropriate fruits on hand can likewise be necessary.

Apples

Bananas

Cherries

Lemons

Limes

Oranges

Pineapples

Strawberries

Fruit juices are utilized as mixers with the alcohol to make different beverages. Plus, having them handy for your non-drinking customers could be just as crucial!

Apple

Cranberry

Grapefruit

Lemon

Lime

Orange

Pineapple

Tomato

Making a few of the more "exotic" beverages calls for the blending of liqueurs in addition to common alcohols and other additives to attain the wanted taste. Liqueurs can likewise be consumed by themselves as shots or an after-dinner nip.

Amaretto (almond)

Blue Curacao (orange)

Chambord (raspberry)

Cointreau (orange)

Creme de Banana (banana)

Creme de Cacao (chocolate)

Creme de Menthe (mint)

Frangelico (hazelnut)

Galliano (herb)

Godiva (chocolate)

Goldschlager (cinnamon)

Grand Marnier (orange)

Jagermeister (herb)

Kahlua (coffee)

Midori (melon)

Rumple Minze (peppermint)

Sambuca (anise)

Schnapps (numerous tastes)

Southern Comfort (peach)

Tia Maria (coffee)

Triple Sec (orange).

There are other mixers you should have handy aside from fruit juices. Numerous beverages use popular soft drinks and other non-conventional ingredients for the beverages.

Angostura Bitters

Lemonade

Cola

Cream

Eggs

Ginger Ale

Grenadine

Ice Cream

Milk

Orange Bitters

Sour Mix

Sprite/7-Up

Tea/Coffee

Water

Soda

Tonic

Lastly, you'll wish to have lots of garnishes around to make your beverages appear enticing and taste yummy.

Cinnamon

Ice

Maraschino Cherries

Nutmeg

Olives (Black and Green)

Salt/Pepper

Sugar Syrup

Tabasco Sauce

Worcestershire Sauce

Stocking a House Bar

When stocking your house bar, you want to bear in mind just how much entertaining you perform and what kinds of beverages your family and friends enjoy. Sure, it may be good to be in a position to produce the ingredients for a Flaming Dr. Pepper, however, if you just have one insane buddy who may ask you for that, the expense of the ingredients may simply surpass the requirement to have them handy.

What should the common house bar have on hand? Well, aside from a healthy supply of beer and wine, here's a good list to begin with.

Gin

Vodka

Rum

Whiskey

Tequila

 Brandy/Cognac.

Fruits are essential as garnishes, having lots of the appropriate fruits handy can likewise be necessary.

Cherries

 Lemons

 Limes

Fruit juices are utilized as mixers with the alcohol to create different drinks. Plus, having them handy for your non-drinking customers could be just as essential!

Apple

Cranberry

Orange

Pineapple

Tomato.

Making a few of the more "exotic" beverages calls for the blending of liqueurs in addition to common liquors and other additives to attain the preferred taste. Liqueurs can likewise be drunk by themselves as shots or an after-dinner nip.

Amaretto (almond)

Creme de Menthe (mint)

Jagermeister (herb)

Kahlua (coffee)

Schnapps (numerous tastes)

Triple Sec (orange)

There are various other mixers you should have on hand aside from fruit juices. Lots of beverages use prominent sodas and other non-conventional ingredients for the beverages.

Cola

 Ginger Ale

 Grenadine

 Sour Mix

Sprite/7-Up

Water

Tonic

Lemon and/or Lime Juice

Lastly, you'll wish to have a lot of garnishes around to make your beverages look attractive and taste yummy.

Ice

 Maraschino Cherries

 Olives (black/green)

Salt/Pepper Sugar

 Tabasco Sauce

Worcestershire Sauce

Obviously, now that you have the ingredients, you'll want the suitable tools to perform the task. The different tools feature glassware, so let's once more see what you'll require for both a commercial and house bar.

Chapter 4: Tools of the Trade

The last thing you wish to take place is to have somebody want a bottle of beer and be lacking a bottle screw. At home or in a business, there are particular tools of the trade that are required in all situations.

Commercial Supplies

Can Opener

Helpful for opening containers of fruit and syrup.

Corkscrew

For opening wine and champagne bottles.

Cloths

Utilized for cleaning surfaces and devices. These need to be damp and not drenched.

Cutting Board

For cutting fruit and various other garnishes-- must be weighty and laminated.

Bar Towels

These are 100% cotton and have actually stitched edges for sturdiness. Utilize these together with cloths to keep things tidy. Make good utilization of times where you have no visitors to clean bottles and clean surfaces.

Bottle screw

For opening bottles.

Bottle Sealers

For maintaining alcohol and other bottled content fresh.

Cocktail Shaker

A shaker is necessary for mixing ingredients in mixed drinks and cocktails. There are lots of cocktail shakers offered. Many do the job. Select one that's appropriate for you.

Electric Blender

Numerous cocktails need a blender to mix the ingredients easily together. These prove extremely helpful for beverages with fruit pieces or ice cream and so on.

Grater

To grate spices such as nutmeg.

Ice Bucket

A metal or insulated ice bucket maintains your ice cool and spotless.

Ice Tongs and Scoops

Utilize these to include ice to beverages without the danger of passing on undesirable bacteria. Never ever manage ice with your hands. Do not utilize glasses as a scoop lest it breaks or chips and leaves undesirable guests in your beverages.

Jigger/Shot Glass

Utilized as a measurement instrument.

Juice Squeezer/Extractor

This is required for acquiring the most juice out of your fruits. It assists to soak citrus fruit in hot water prior to squeezing.

Bar Spoon

A bar spoon has a lengthy handle and a muddler end that is going to permit you to blend and measure ingredients in addition to crushing garnishes.

Measuring Cups

Generally, these ought to be glass or chrome with incremented measurements inscribed up the side. These are required for precise measurement. They typically come with a set of measuring spoons which are required for some tinier amounts.

Mixing Glass

A mixing glass works for long beverages where it is needed to blend the ingredients without shaking.

Sharp Knife

For chopping fruit and garnishes.

Strainer

This gets rid of the ice and fruit pulp from juices. This might feature a cocktail shaker.

Glasses and Containers

There are numerous kinds of glassware of various sizes and shapes all serving their own function. Knowing which beverages belong to which glass is helpful to both you and your customers. They get a better beverage which consequently reflects back on you and your facility.

Ensure all glassware is washed and clean before serving it to your customers. Wash glasses with warm water and a tiny quantity of detergent, but not soap. Wash them later on with fresh, cold water and polish them with an appropriate fabric. Hold glasses by the bottom or stem of the glass to avoid fingerprints.

The following are all the glasses you are going to require in a commercial bar.

Beer Mug

A conventional beer container-- generally 16 ounces.

Brandy snifter

The design of this glass focuses the alcoholic smells to the top of the glass as your hands heat the brandy. Common Size: 17.5 oz.

Champagne Flute

A tulip-shaped glass created to flaunt the bubbles of the wine as they brush against the side of the glass and expand into a gleaming pattern. Normally 6 ounces Cocktail glass.

This glass has a triangle-bowl style with a lengthy stem, and is utilized for a vast array of straight-up (without ice) cocktails, featuring martinis, manhattans, metropolitans, and gimlets. It is likewise referred to as a martini glass. Normal Size: 4-12 oz.

Coffee Mug

Conventional mug utilized for hot coffee-- generally 12 to 16 ounces.

Collins glass

Formed similarly to a highball glass, just taller, the Collins glass was initially utilized for the line of Collins gin beverages, and is now additionally typically utilized for sodas, alcoholic juice, and tropical/exotic juices like Mai Tai's. Common Size: 14 oz.

Cordial Glass

Little and stemmed glasses utilized for offering tiny portions of your favorite alcohol after a meal. Generally, 2 ounces.

Highball glass

A straight-sided glass, typically a classy way to serve numerous kinds of alcoholic drinks, like those served on the rocks, shots, and mixer combined liquor drinks (ie. gin and tonic). Common Size: 8-12 oz.

Hurricane Glass

A high, elegantly cut glass called after its hurricane lamp-like shape and utilized for exotic or tropic beverages. 15 ounces.

Margarita/Coupette glass

This somewhat bigger and rounded approach to a cocktail glass has a broad-rim for holding salt, suitable for margaritas. It is likewise utilized in daiquiris and other fruit beverages. Common Size: 12 oz.

Mason Jar

These are big square containers and are helpful in maintaining their contents sealed in an impermeable environment. Generally, these are utilized for home canning and are approximately 16 ounces.

Old-fashioned glass

A short, round so called "rocks" glass, appropriate for mixed drinks or alcohol served on the rocks, or "with a splash." Common Size: 8-10 oz.

Parfait Glass

This glass has a comparable inward curve to that of a hurricane glass, however, with a steeper outwards rim and bigger rounded pot. These are frequently utilized for beverages consisting of fruit or ice cream. 12 ounces

Pousse-cafe glass

A narrow glass basically utilized for pousse cafés and additional layered dessert beverages. Its shape boosts the ease of layering ingredients. The common size is 6 oz.

Punch Bowl

A big round bowl utilized for punches or big mixes.

Red wine glass

A transparent, thin, stemmed glass with a round pot tapering inward at the rim. Common Size: 8 oz.

Sherry Glass

This is the favored glass for aperitifs, ports, and sherry. This has a slim taper and is generally around 2 ounces.

Shot glass

A shot glass is a little glass appropriate for vodka, scotch and other alcohol. Numerous "shot" cocktails likewise require shot glasses. Common Size: 1.5 oz.

Whiskey Sour Glass

This kind of glass is likewise referred to as a Delmonico glass. It has a stemmed broad opening comparable to a champagne flute and holds about 5 ounces.

White wine glass

A transparent, slim, stemmed glass with a lengthened oval bowl tapering inward at the rim. Common Size: 12.5 oz.

Home Bar

Stocking tools for a house bar is going to need much less supplies, however, there are a couple of staples you are going to absolutely wish to have.

Can Opener

Beneficial for opening cans of fruit juices.

Corkscrew

For opening wine and champagne bottles.

Cloths

For cleaning surfaces and tools. These need to be moist and not drenched.

Cutting Board

A hefty, laminated cutting board is ideal for cutting fruit and other garnishes.

Bottle screw

For opening bottles.

Cocktail Shaker

This is utilized for mixing ingredients in mixed drinks and cocktails.

Electric Blender

Numerous cocktails need a blender to mix the ingredients effortlessly together. This works for beverages with fruit bits or ice cream and so on.

Ice Bucket

A metal or insulated ice bucket maintains your ice chilly and spotless.

Ice Tongs and Scoops

Tongs are utilized to include ice to beverages.

Jigger/Shot Glass

This is utilized as a measurement tool.

Sharp Knife

For chopping fruit and garnishes.

Glass and Containers:

Beer Mug

16 ounces-- conventional beer container.

Champagne Flute

6 ounces-- tulip-shaped glass created to flaunt the bubbles from the champagne.

Cocktail glass

This glass has a triangle-bowl style with a lengthy stem, and is utilized for a vast array of straight-up (without ice) mixed drinks, consisting of martinis, manhattans, metropolitans, and gimlets - additionally referred to as a martini glass. Common Size: 4-12 oz.

Collins glass

Formed in a similar way to a highball glass, just taller, the Collins glass was initially utilized for the line of Collins gin beverages, and is now likewise frequently utilized for sodas, alcoholic juice, and tropical/exotic juices like Mai Tai's. Common Size: 14 oz.

Highball glass

A straight-sided glass, frequently a sophisticated method to serve lots of kinds of cocktails, like those served on the rocks, shots, and mixer combined liquor drinks (i.e. gin and tonic). Common Size: 8-12 oz.

Hurricane Glass

This is a high glass with a hurricane lamp shape utilized for unusual or tropic beverages.

Margarita/Coupette glass

This somewhat bigger and rounded approach to a mixed drink glass has a broad-rim for holding salt, perfect for margaritas. It is likewise utilized in daiquiris and other fruit beverages. Common Size: 12 oz.

Old-fashioned glass

A short, round so called "rocks" glass, appropriate for mixed drinks or alcohol served on the rocks, or "with a splash." Common Size: 8-10 oz.

Red wine glass

A transparent, slim, stemmed glass with a round bowl tapering inward at the rim. Common Size: 8 oz.

Shot glass

This is a little glass ideal for vodka, scotch and other liquors. Lots of "shot" cocktails likewise require shot glasses.
Common Size: 1.5 oz.

Whether you are at house or at work, it's necessary to master a few of the fundamental methods of bartending before you begin.

Chapter 5: Fundamental Methods

Making mixed drinks can be simple or creative depending upon the individual, their tastes and how far they wish to do things. Typically the very first lesson of Bartending School teaches the fundamental abilities from shaking to pouring over a spoon. The majority of people can quickly get by with these methods in an expert circumstance.

Shaking

Shaking is the technique by which you utilize a cocktail shaker to blend ingredients together and cool them at the same time. The aim is to practically freeze the beverage while breaking down and integrating the ingredients.

Typically, this is performed with ice cubes put into the shaker about 3/4 of the way to the top. After that pour in the ingredients, hold the shaker in both hands with one hand on top and one hand upholding the foundation.

Give the shaker a brief, sharp, quick shake. DO NOT rock your cocktail to sleep. When water has actually started to condense on the surface of the shaker, the cocktail is cooled and prepared to be strained.

Straining

The majority of cocktail shakers are offered with a build-in strainer or hawthorn strainer. When a beverage requires straining, make sure you have actually utilized ice cubes, as crushed ice has a tendency to obstruct the strainer of a basic shaker. If a beverage is needed shaken with crushed ice (i.e. Shirley Temple), it is to be offered unstrained.

Stirring

You are able to stir cocktails successfully with a metal or glass rod in a mixing glass. In case you utilize ice, utilize them to stop dilution and strain the contents into a glass when the surface of the mixing glass starts to gather condensation.

Muddling

To draw out the most taste from particular fresh ingredients like fruit or mint garnishes, you need to squash the ingredient with the muddler on the rear end of your bar spoon, or with a pestle.

Blending

An electrical blender is typically required for recipes consisting of fruit or other ingredients that do not deteriorate by shaking. Blending is a fantastic method to blend these ingredients with others developing a smooth, prepared to serve blend.

Some recipes require ice to be put in the blender, in which instance you would utilize an appropriate quantity of crushed ice to generate a smooth, pleasant-tasting beverage.

Building

When creating a cocktail, the ingredients are poured into the glass wherein the cocktail is going to be offered. Normally, the ingredients are drifting on top of each other, yet sometimes, a swizzle stick is placed in the glass, enabling the ingredients to be blended.

Layering

To layer or float an ingredient like cream liquor on top of another, utilize the rounded, rear section of a spoon and rest it versus the interior of a glass. Gradually pour the alcohol down the spoon and into the glass. The ingredient ought to run down the interior of the glass and stay separated from the ingredient beneath it.

Flaming

Flaming is the technique by which a cocktail or liquor is ignited, generally, to boost the taste of a beverage. It ought to be tried with care, and for the above reason only, not to merely appear cool.

Some liquor is going to ignite rather quickly if their proof is high. Warming a tiny amount of the alcohol in a spoon is going to induce the alcohol to gather at the top, which can then be quickly lit. You are able to then pour this over the ready ingredients.

Do not include alcohol to ignited beverages and do not leave them unwatched. Light them where they present no threat to anyone else, and make sure no things can possibly enter into contact with any flames from the beverage. Constantly snuff out a flaming beverage prior to consuming it.

There's absolutely nothing more dismal than a "frou-frou" beverage that has no decor to it. Here are a few of the more prominent decor methods.

Chapter 6: Embellishing Your Cocktails

Decoration of a beverage is going to typically include a couple of fruits, herbs, or cherry garnishes that either complement the taste of the beverage, contrast with the color, or both. It is essential that you stay clear of overpowering the beverage. When garnishing with fruit, be cautious with the size. In case it is too slim, it's flimsy and unexciting. A too-thick piece can unbalance the appearance and even taste of the cocktail.

Citrus Twists

To create a citrus twist, cut a slim piece of the fruit crosswise and merely twist to serve on the side of a glass or in it.

Citrus Peel Spirals

To create a spiral of citrus peel, utilize a parer or veggie peeler to remove the skin, operating in a circular motion. Make sure not to cut into the bitter pith.

Citrus Peel Knots

Utilize strips of peel and cautiously bind each strip into a knot. Drop it into the beverage for a great garnish.

Mixed drink Sticks

These incredibly helpful wooden cocktail sticks are required for spearing through bits of fruit and cherries. These are not reusable. Plastic mixed drink sticks, nevertheless, are reusable given they are cleaned and boiled.

Frosting/Rimming

Margaritas and other cocktails frequently require the rim of the glass to be covered with salt, sugar, or some other ingredient. This is referred to as icing or rimming. The simplest method to perform this is to rub the rim of the glass with a piece of citrus fruit and after that dip the very edge of the rim into a little pot loaded with sugar or salt.

Maraschino Cherries

You need to constantly have an abundant supply of red maraschino cherries to adorn your mixed drinks with. These are the most commonly used for decorations, along with being available in several colors and tastes.

Olives or Onions

Martinis are typically garnished with olives or cocktail onions. Just skewer one or two with a toothpick and drop into the beverage.

Straws

Straws are vital and match lots of mixed drinks. These, naturally, should never ever be re-used.

Before we carry on to the good part-- recipes-- we want to attend to the concern of bar safety and cleanliness.

Chapter 7: Hygiene and Safety

Here a couple of rules to bear in mind relating to hygiene and safety in a bar, whether it be at house or at work. While the majority of these tips may be common sense, they bear a notation within this book for the safety of you, your friends and/or your patrons!

Constantly be neat, tidy, and diplomatic. Constantly wash or clean bar tools such as cocktail shakers and strainers after every usage-- even in between beverages.

Constantly wash and dry your hands regularly-- specifically after contact with citrus fruit and juices. This aids to protects against scaling of the hands and infection from dermatitis.

Take great care of your hands-- particularly your fingernails as these are constantly visible. Keep nails short. If you utilize nail polish, utilize neutral colors so the focus is on you and your work rather than your fingernails.

Generally, it is frowned upon to smoke or sip while operating behind a bar. Many individuals see it as unhygienic. In some locations, it is additionally unlawful.

When uncorking the champagne, attempt to stop the pop of the cork. While this is typically related to champagne, it can be a hazardous practice if the cork should end up being errant.

When utilizing a soda siphon, manage it by the plastic or metal part only. This is the most hygienic approach to pouring a soda. Never ever fill a glass to the verge. This promotes spilling and makes the whole bar unhygienic and unpleasant.

Now, let's take a look at a few of the more typical beverage recipes.

Chapter 8: Drink recipes

There are a multitude of beverages out there created in somebody's basement or kitchen when there were simply a couple of drops of alcohol left and some kind of mixer. Others have actually been produced by bored bartenders who believed particular mixes may taste excellent together. Still, others are staples that are bought almost every day in a bar.

I can't include all the beverage recipes, however here are a few of the most prominent ones.

Alabama Slammer

1/2 oz amaretto almond liqueur

1/2 oz Southern Comfort ® peach liqueur

1/2 oz sloe gin

1 splash orange juice

1 splash sweet and sour mix

Pour above ingredients into a stainless-steel shaker over ice and shake up until entirely cold. Strain into an old-fashioned glass and offer.

Amaretto Sour

1 1/2 oz amaretto almond liqueur

1 - 2 splashes sweet and sour mix

Pour the amaretto liqueur into a cocktail shaker half-filled with ice. Include a splash or more of sweet and sour blend, and shake properly. Strain or pour into an old-fashioned glass, decorate with a maraschino cherry and a piece of orange, and offer.

Brandy Alexander

1 1/2 oz brandy

1 oz dark crème de cacao

1 oz half-and-half

1/4 tsp grated nutmeg

In a shaker half-filled with ice, blend the brandy, crème de cacao, and half-and-half. Shake properly. Strain into a mixed drink glass and decorate with the nutmeg.

Bloody Mary

1 1/2 oz vodka

3 oz tomato juice

1 dash lemon juice

1/2 tsp Worcestershire sauce

2 - 3 drops Tabasco ® sauce

1 lime wedge

Shake all ingredients (except lime wedge) with ice and strain into an old-fashioned glass over ice cubes. Include salt and pepper to taste. Include the wedge of lime and offer.

Blue Hawaiian

1 oz light rum

1 cherry

2 oz pineapple juice

1 oz Blue Curacao liqueur

1 oz cream of coconut

1 slice pineapple

Mix light rum, blue Curacao, pineapple juice, and cream of coconut with a single cup of ice in an electrical blender at high speed. Pour components into a highball glass. Embellish with the piece of pineapple and a cherry.

Cosmopolitan

1 oz vodka

 1/2 oz triple sec

1/2 oz lime juice

1/2 oz cranberry juice

Shake vodka, triple sec, lime and cranberry juice intensely in a shaker with ice. Strain into a martini glass, decorate with a lime wedge on the rim, and offer.

Fuzzy Navel

1 part peach schnapps

1 part orange juice

1 part lemonade

Mix equivalent parts of every ingredient in a highball glass, cover with ice, and offer.

Gibson

1 1/2 oz gin

3/4 oz vermouth

2 cocktail onions

Whisk gin and vermouth over ice within a mixing glass. Strain into a cocktail glass. Include the cocktail onions and offer.

Gimlet

2 oz gin

1/2 oz lime juice

1 lime wedge

Pour the gin and lime juice into a blending glass half-filled with ice. Whisk properly. Strain into a cocktail glass and decorate with the lime wedge.

Harvey Wallbanger

1 oz vodka

1/2 oz Galliano ® herbal liqueur

 4 oz orange juice

Pour vodka and orange juice into a Collins glass over ice and whisk. Float Galliano on top and offer.

Kamikaze

1 oz vodka

 1 oz triple sec

 1 oz lime juice

Shake all ingredients with ice, strain into an old-fashioned glass over ice, and offer.

Lemon Drop

1/2 oz vodka

1/2 oz lemon juice

1 sugar cube

Include sugar to the rim of an old-fashioned glass, and drop a cube or package of sugar into the base of the glass. Pour vodka and lemon juice into a stainless-steel shaker over ice, and shake up until totally frosty. Pour into the ready old-fashioned glass, and offer.

Long Island Ice Tea

1 part vodka

1 part tequila

1 part rum

1 part gin

1 part triple sec

1 1/2 parts sweet and sour mix

1 splash cola

Mix ingredients together over ice within a glass. Pour into a shaker and deliver one vigorous shake. Put back into the glass and ensure there is a dash of fizz on top. Decorate with lemon.

Mai Tai

1 oz light rum

1/2 oz crème de almond

 1/2 oz triple sec

sweet and sour mix

pineapple juice

1/2 oz Myer's ® dark rum

Pour light rum, crème de almond and triple sec, in order, right into a Collins glass. Nearly fill with equivalent parts of sweet and sour blend and pineapple juice. Include dark rum, a big straw, and offer unstirred.

Margarita

1 1/2 oz tequila

1/2 oz triple sec

1 oz lime juice

salt

Scrub the rim of a mixed drink glass with lime juice, and soak in salt. Shake all ingredients with ice, strain into the glass, and offer.

Mojito

3 fresh mint sprigs

2 tsp sugar

3 tbsp fresh lime juice

1 1/2 oz light rum club soda

In a high slim glass, squash part of the mint with a fork to coat the interior. Include the sugar and lime juice and whisk completely. Cover with ice. Include rum and blend. Round off with cooled club soda (or seltzer). Include a lemon piece and the remaining mint, and offer.

Mudslide

1 1/2 oz Bailey's ® Irish cream

1/2 oz Kahlua ® coffee liqueur

Pour Hershey's chocolate syrup across the interior rim of a rocks glass. Load with ice, include ingredients, and offer.

Old Fashioned

2 oz mixed scotch

1 sugar cube

1 dash bitters

1 slice of lemon

1 cherry

1 slice of orange

Mix the sugar cube, bitters, and 1 tsp. water in an old-fashioned glass. Jumble well, include mixed whiskey, and mix. Include a twist of lemon peel and ice. Include pieces of orange and lemon and cover with the cherry. Offer with a swizzle stick.

Pina Colada

3 oz light rum

3 tbsp coconut milk

3 tbsp crushed pineapples

Place all ingredients into an electrical blender with 2 cups of smashed ice. Mix at high speed for a brief period of time. Strain into a Collins glass and offer with a straw

Rob Roy

1 1/2 oz Scotch whisky

3/4 oz sweet vermouth

Whisk ingredients with ice, strain into a mixed drink glass, and offer.

Salty Dog

5 oz grapefruit juice

1 1/2 oz gin

1/4 tsp salt

Put all ingredients over ice in a highball glass. Whisk properly and offer. (Vodka might be alternative to gin, if chosen.).

Seabreeze

1 1/2 oz vodka

4 oz cranberry juice

1 oz grapefruit juice.

Pour vodka accross ice into a highball glass. Include mixers. The beverage might be spruced up with a wedge of lime.

Sex on the Beach

1 oz vodka

3/4 oz peach schnapps

cranberry juice

grapefruit juice.

Include vodka and peach schnapps to a highball glass. Load with equivalent amounts of cranberry juice and grapefruit juice, and whisk.

Sloe Comfortable Screw

3 oz sloe gin

3 oz Southern Comfort ® peach liqueur

3 oz orange juice

3 oz vodka.

Whisk or shake ingredients & offer with ice.

Strawberry Daiquiri

1/2 oz strawberry schnapps

1 oz light rum

1 oz lime juice

1 tsp powdered sugar

1 oz strawberries.

Shake all ingredients with ice, strain into a mixed drink glass, and offer.

Tequila Sunrise

1 shot tequila

Orange juice

2 dashes grenadine syrup.

Pour tequila in a highball glass with ice, and cover with orange juice. Whisk. Include grenadine by tilting the glass and putting grenadine down side by turning the bottle vertically really rapidly. The grenadine ought to go straight to the base and after that, rise gradually through the beverage.

Tom Collins

2 oz gin

1 oz lemon juice

1 tsp superfine sugar

3 oz club soda

1 maraschino cherry

1 slice of orange.

In a shaker half-filled with ice, blend the gin, lemon juice, and sugar. Shake properly. Strain into a collins glass nearly loaded with ice. Include the club soda. Whisk and decorate with the cherry and the orange slice.

Whiskey Sour

2 oz mixed whiskey

juice of 1/2 lemons

1/2 tsp powdered sugar

1 cherry

1/2 slice of lemon.

Shake combined scotch, juice of lemon, and powdered sugar with ice and strain into a whiskey sour glass. Embellish with the half-slice of lemon, cover with the cherry, and offer.

The trend towards martini drinking is ending up being progressively popular. Want some awesome martini recipes? That's the next part!

Chapter 9: Martinis Galore!

Common Gin Martini

A lot of people argue that the gin martini is the only blend fitting to don the name "martini," and all other mixed drinks are shams.

Ingredients:

- 6 ounces of gin

- 5 drops of dry vermouth

- 2 little twists of lemon rind

- 2 olives

The mix:

- Fill up a glass martini shaker about 3/4 with split, tidy ice

- Put your gin into the shaker and allow it stand for a minute. Count down from sixty to zero.

- Shake, shake, and shake. Approximately fifteen, energetic, diagonal shakes ought to suffice.

- Place that shaker down and get 2 well-chilled martini glasses from the refrigerator or freezer. Enable the shaker to rest for approximately another minute.

- Into every glass drop two drops of vermouth (the fifth drop is only for good fortune).

- Every glass receives a twist and an olive (the olive could be optional).

- Strain your really cold gin into every glass.

Common Vodka Martini

Although this martini is going to definitely qualify as a common martini, you'll frequently discover that every bartender is going to produce the beverage with a minor (or maybe not so minor) variation.

Ingredients:

- 3 ounces of vodka.

- 1 teaspoon vermouth.

- 3 olives.

The mix:

- Pour your vodka into a well-chilled shaker and allow it to stand for a minute. Count down from sixty to zero.

- Whilst counting down, drop your vermouth into an icy martini glass, swirl the vermouth across the glass and after that pour it out.

- Shake, shake, and shake. About fifteen, energetic, angled shakes followed by swirling the shaker a couple of times.

- Strain your freezing vodka into your glass.

- Spear your olives and carefully move them into the glass.

Chocolate Martini:

1 1/2 shots chocolate liqueur

 1 1/2 shots crème de cacao

1/2 shot vodka

2 1/2 shots half-and-half.

Combine all ingredients in a shaker with ice, shake and pour into a cooled mixed drink glass.

Apple Martini:

1 part vodka

1 part DeKuyper ® Sour Apple Pucker schnapps

 1 part apple juice.

Pour all ingredients into a shaker. Shake properly and strain into a Martini glass.

Dirty Martini

Ingredients:

- 6 ounces of vodka.

- 1 teaspoon of vermouth.

- 6 olives.

- Toasted almond slivers.

The mix:

- Pour your Vodka into a well-chilled shaker and allow it to stand for half a minute.

- While counting down, drop your vermouth into 2 icy martini glasses, swirl the vermouth across the glasses and after that pour it out.

- Shake, shake, and shake. About twenty, energetic, angled shakes followed by swirling the shaker a couple of times.

- Strain your frosty vodka into your glasses.

- Place an almond sliver into every packed olive and spear 3 per toothpick.

- Spear your olives and lightly move them into the glass.

Lemon Martini:

Ingredients:

- 4 ounces of vodka.

- 1/2 teaspoon of dry vermouth.

- 1 lemon twist.

- 1 thin lemon slice.

- 1 teaspoon Limoncello.

The mix:

- Rim your icy martini glass with Lemon Twist cocktail candy and put back in the freezer up until required.

- Pour your vodka, vermouth and Limoncello into a shaker 3/4 loaded with ice.

- 20 lively shakes (no stirring possibility on this one) ought to blend it well.

- Recover your martini glass and strain the blend into it.

- Cut your lemon slice halfway and drop it on to the edge of the glass.

- Include your lemon twist.

The Boardroom Smoky Martini.

Ingredients:

- 1/2 ounce dry vermouth.

- 4 ounces of gin.

- 2 tablespoons Scotch (10 years old is preferred). You are able to try out any great, single malt Scotch.

- 2 lemon twists.

The mix:

- Pour your vermouth and gin into a shaker 1/2 filled with crushed ice.

- Shake, shake, and shake for a complete minute. You might additionally stir for a complete 2 minutes.

- Include your Scotch and whisk 4 times in a counter-clockwise movement.

- Strain your smoky flavored martini into 2 well-chilled martini glasses.

- Every glass receives a twist.

Hey Sweetie Martini

This is a really sweet martini. This is a fantastic option for a Cosmo enthusiast, like the person you'll be wowing with this easy to mix martini.

Ingredients:

- 7 ounces of freezing vodka.

- 1 ounce of room temperature Chambord.

- 1 teaspoon of honey.

The mix:

- Heat your honey (a little) and whisk it into your Chambord.

- Pour your vodka into a shaker 3/4 loaded with crushed ice.

- Shake, shake, shake.

- Include your honey-infused Chambord and whisk 3 times.

- Strain your fluid into 2 icy martini glasses.

Key Lime Martini

Ingredients:

- 4 ounces Key Lime Vodka.

- 2 ounces vodka.

- 2 tablespoons of fresh lime juice.

- 1 tablespoon of cool whip.

- 2 martini glasses rimmed with lime cocktail candy sugar.

- 2 incredibly thin cuts of lime.

The mix:

- All of your vodka and 1 tablespoon of cool whip enters into a shaker that is 3/4 filled with crushed ice.

- Shake for a great minute.

- Allow your shaker to rest for thirty seconds.

- Include 1 tablespoon of the lime juice to the shaker and provide additional 10 shakes.

- Strain into your 2 frosty martini glasses.

- Include 1/2 of the lingering lime juice to every glass, and cover each with a little bit of the lingering cool whip.

- Float a lime piece on every glass.

Valentine Martini

Ingredients:

- 5 ounces of freezing Chopin vodka.

- 5 ounces of chilled ice wine.

- 11 green seedless grapes at room temperature.

- 1 tablespoon of fresh lemon juice.

- 2 frozen green grapes.

The mix:

- Include all of your fluid ingredients to a blender or food processor.

- Strain into a cocktail shaker 1/2 filled with crushed ice.

- Shake for a complete minute.

- Strain your fantastic martini into 2 icy cocktail glasses.

For those of you who are "shot" lovers, here is a distinct part that follows with some fundamental shot recipes.

Chapter 10: Hit me Sargeant

Shots are more than merely a pour of alcohol into a shot glass. Nowadays, shots have actually risen to an art form. Here are a few of the more prominent ones.

B-52

1/3 shot Kahlua ® coffee liqueur

1/3 shot amaretto almond liqueur

1/3 shot Bailey's ® Irish cream

Thoroughly layer ingredients, in order, into a shot glass; kahlua, amaretto, and after that Irish cream.

Blow Job

1/4 oz Bailey's ® Irish cream

1/2 oz amaretto almond liqueur

Pour liqueurs into a shot glass and cover with whipped cream. Have a person put their hands behind their back, and after that; pick up the loaded shot glass with their mouth, lean head back, and drink.

Body Shots

1 oz vodka

1 package sugar

1 lemon wedge

Utilizing a partner of the reverse sex, lick their neck to dampen. Pour the package of sugar onto their neck. Put a wedge of lemon in their mouth with the skin pointed inward. You initially lick the sugar from their neck, and after that shoot the vodka, and then suck the lemon from their mouth (while carefully holding back of their neck).

Buttery Nipple

1 oz DeKuyper ® Buttershots liqueur

1/2 oz Irish cream

Pour buttershots into a cooled shot glass. Thoroughly layer or float the irish cream on top, and offer.

Chocolate Cake

1/2 oz Frangelico ® hazelnut liqueur

1/2 oz vodka

Sugar

Incorporate vodka and Frangelico to a shaker with ice. Shake. Decorate with a sugar-coated lemon. Shoot the drink, as you would tequila.

Flaming Dr. Pepper

3/4 shot amaretto almond liqueur

1/4 oz 151 proof rum

1/2 glass beer

Load a shot glass about 3/4 full with amaretto and cover it with plenty of 151 proof rum to be capable to burn.

Put the shot glass in another glass and load the external glass with beer (right up to the level of the shot glass).

Spark the amaretto/151 and allow it to burn for some time. Blow it out (or leave it burning, in case you're gutsy - not advised) and slam it. Tastes much like Dr. Pepper.

Jager Bomb

1 can Red Bull ® energy drink

1 oz Jagermeister ® herbal liqueur

Pour red bull into a pint glass. Drop in a shot glass loaded with Jagermeister, and down.

Jello Shots

1 package watermelon jell-o

1 cup boiling water

1 cup Malibu ® coconut rum

Blend warm water and jello. Include rum. Pour into 2 ounce cups. Offer after the jello has actually set.

Kamikaze

1 part vodka

1 part triple sec

1 part Rose's ® lime juice

Shake properly with ice and strain blend into a shot glass.

Liquid Cocaine

1/2 oz Bacardi ® 151 rum

1/2 oz Goldschlager ® cinnamon schnapps

1/2 oz Jagermeister ® herbal liqueur

Pour ingredients, as noted above into a big shot glass and shoot.

Purple Hooter

1/2 oz vodka

1/2 oz Chambord ® raspberry liqueur

1 splash 7-Up ® soda

Pour ingredients into a stainless-steel shaker across the ice. Shake up until ice cold. Strain into a big shot glass, and offer.

Red Headed Slut

1 oz peach schnapps

1 oz Jagermeister ® natural liqueur

cranberry juice

Cool and offer.

Scooby Snack

1/2 oz Malibu ® coconut rum

1/2 oz crème de bananas

1/2 oz Midori ® melon liqueur

1/2 oz pineapple juice

1 1/2 oz whipped cream

Pour rum, crème de banana, melon liqueur and pineapple juice into a stainless steel shaker across the ice. Include whipped cream, and shake; up until properly blended and adequately cooled. Strain into an old-fashioned glass and shoot.

Surfer On Acid

1/2 oz Jagermeister ® organic liqueur

1/2 oz Malibu ® coconut rum

1/2 oz pineapple juice

Pour ingredients into a stainless-steel shaker across the ice and shake up until entirely cold. Strain into a big shot or old-fashioned glass and shoot.

There are numerous drink recipes available; space stops me from including them all. You can discover almost every recipe you require at drinksmixer.com.

Being an excellent bartender, however, is a lot more than merely blending excellent drinks. You need to develop your character and provide individuals with something to talk about. How about a couple of awesome bar tricks?

Chapter 11: Bar Tricks

Bar Trick # 1 Olive in Brandy Snifter.

Ingredients: 1 olive and 1 brandy snifter.

Goal: Place olive in a brandy snifter.

Scenario: You can not touch the olive with your body (hands, mouth, and so on). You may not scoop the olive with the snifter. You can not roll olive off of bar into a snifter.

Answer: With the olive on the bar. Put the brandy snifter across the olive to ensure that the open end of the snifter is encompassing the olive. Gradually turn the brandy snifter around the olive. The olive is going to roll around the interior walls of the snifter (centrifugal force). When the olive is rotating around the center of the snifter, turn the snifter upright and put on the bar. Gather your earnings!

Tips: Practice this bar trick prior to making any bets. The olive tends to come out of snifter when turning upright. After a bit of practice, you are going to be a pro.

Bar Trick # 2 Humiliate your Friends.

Ingredients: 1 bar napkin, and 1 pen/pencil.

Goal: Humiliate your friends and other folks.

Scenario: On a bar napkin jot down the following:

I AM WE TODD IT I AM SOFA KING WE TODD IT

Ask your buddies to carry on reading out loud up until they get the idea.

Continue to locate fresh victims.

Additional Bonus: Old victims are going to laugh at fresh victims.

Bar Trick # 3 The Race!

Ingredients: 3 shots of _____, and 3 pints of beer.

Goal: Get a free round of beverages.

Scenario: Inform your victim that you are going to drink your 3 pints of beer quicker then they are able to drink their 3 little shots of _____.

Player's rules: You may not touch the other player's glass or shot.

Answer: Begin drinking your beer. Your victim is going to take their initial shot. As quickly as you wrap up drinking your initial beer, put your empty pint over your victim's 3rd shot. Go slowly and enjoy your free beverages. Your victim can not touch your glass, check out the rule above. You are the winner!

Bar Trick # 4 The old "2 quarters trick?"

Ingredients: 2 quarters, and one target.

Goal: To get a free beverage.

Scenario: On the bar put 2 quarters heads up. Ask your target, "What do you see." The typical response is, "Two heads!" or "Two quarters." Gradually begin nodding your head in agreement and with your palm up point to the two quarters and state, "I see two cents, hey, if I'm wrong, will you purchase me a beverage." Pressure them for a response, many people are going to say, "Sure." Now say, "I'm wrong." Enjoy your free beverage.

Extra Bonus: When the beverage is empty, locate a brand-new target.

Bar Trick # 5 The Fifty cent beverage.

Ingredients: 1 Target with a fresh beverage, 1 cocktail napkin, 2 quarters.

Goal: To get an inexpensive beverage.

Scenario: Taking target's beverage and getting rid of any straws or umbrellas. Cover victim's drink with the cocktail napkin. Say to your victim, "I wager you fifty cents that without touching the glass or the napkin or any straws and so on, I can drink that whole beverage."

Press the two quarters towards the victim while wagering, point to the glass and the napkin. Continue to claim, "I will not touch anything!"

Bring up the point about perhaps placing a straw through the napkin and reiterate, "I will not touch anything!"

Answer: When they quit, gradually remove the napkin and take pleasure in the beverage as you press the fifty cents to the victim. Make sure to inform the victim they won and hand them their fifty cents. The $4.00 beverage simply cost you fifty cents! Enjoy your inexpensive beverage!

Bar Trick # 6 Salt & Pepper

Ingredients: 1 target, 1 salt package, 1 pepper package, and 1 little plastic comb.

Goal: To get a free beverage.

Scenario: Make a little hill of salt on the bar, approximately the size of a quarter. Then spray a touch of pepper on top of the salt. Wager your victim one beverage that they can not get the pepper off, without disrupting the salt.

Answer: Take your plastic comb and comb your hair a couple of times. After that hold the comb over the salt & pepper. The static electricity is going to draw the pepper off the salt.

Keep in mind: This trick will just work when the humidity levels are low.

Bar Trick # 7 Sugar Cubes

Ingredients: 1 target, 2 sugar cubes, 1 lighter, and 1 ashtray.

Goal: To get a free beverage.

Scenario: Hand somebody a sugar cube and a lighter. Wager them a beverage that they can not light the sugar cube on fire. They are going to attempt to light it on fire by putting the flame under it. They are going to get the cube to smoke, char and smolder, however, it is not going to combust.

Answer: Rub your sugar cube in an ashtray to get some ashes on it. Hold the flame to the sugar cube, it ought to light right up.

Keep in mind: Practice this a couple of times before you begin making bets.

Bar Trick # 8 Ice Cubes

Ingredients: 1 target, 2 ice cubes, a bit of salt, and 2 pieces of human hair (about 6 to 8 inches long).

Goal: To receive a free beverage.

Scenario: Wager somebody they can not pick up an ice cube with one piece of human hair. The typical individual is going to attempt to twist and tie the hair around the ice cube. Others will attempt to simply raise it up. Nevertheless, they will not have the ability to get the ice cube off the bar.

Answer: Put the ice cube on the bar, take a strand of human hair and put it over the top of the ice. After that, take a little salt and spray it on top of the hair and ice cube. The salt is going to cause the ice cube to re-freeze around the hair. In a couple of seconds, you are going to have the ability to carefully raise the ice cube off of the bar.

Keep in mind: Practice this a couple of times before you begin making bets.

Bar Trick # 9 The Switch

Ingredients: 2 similar shot glasses, 1 non-porous paper (playing card, over-sized matchbook, and so on), water, and your choice of alcohol (bourbon, scotch, and so on).

Goal: Challenge your buddies.

Scenario: Fill one shot glass with water and the other with, let's say, bourbon. The challenge is to put the bourbon in the glass that has the water and the water in the glass that has the bourbon without utilizing some other containers including your mouth (or anybody else's mouth).

Answer: Put the non-porous paper (playing card) on top of the shot of water. Flip the card and water shot upside down cautiously. The paper is going to remain connected to the shot on its own accord.

Now, put the water shot glass and card on the shot of bourbon. Gradually and cautiously pull the paper out simply far enough to make a really little opening in between the two glasses. Water, being heavier than alcohol is going to stream to the bourbon glass and displace the bourbon into the water glass. You have simply performed the switch.

If you are genuinely proficient at this bar trick, you are going to have the ability to replace the paper in between the two shot glasses and get rid of the bourbon and place it back on the bar.

Keep in mind: Ensure the opening in between the glasses is really little. A big opening is going to induce the water and alcohol to blend.

Bar Trick # 10 Smoke on the water.

Ingredients: 1 glass, a matchbook, 6 quarters, and an ashtray with water.

Goal: Get a free beverage.

Scenario: Wager your buddies one beverage that you can get the water out of the ashtray utilizing just the ingredients mentioned and without moving or tipping the ashtray.

Answer: Ensure that the ashtray is filled with at most a quarter-inch of water. Stack the quarters in the center of the ashtray so the top 2 quarters are above the water. Put 4 unlit matches on top of the quarters. Light the matches and promptly cover the flame and quarters with the glass. The water is going to be drawn into the glass. Gather your bets.

Bar Trick # 11 The Wish in a Bottle

Ingredients: 1 recently emptied bottle of Grand Marnier, a matchbook, a cork, a straw, and a sword cocktail pick.

Goal: To play with fire while making a wish.

Scenario: Get your buddies to make a wish. Let them know if the sword sticks in the ceiling, then their wish is going to come to life.

Answer: Take a recently emptied Grand Marnier bottle and place a cork in it. Put the bottle under boiling water for about 10 minutes. While the bottle is warming up, take a straw and fold it in half. Take your sword pick and stick it through the fold in the straw. The straw ought to be folded back over the handle of the sword pick.

When the bottle is prepared, cautiously get rid of the cork so the heated gas in the bottle does not leave. Rapidly place the straw and the sword in the bottle with the pointer of the sword pick pointing out the opening of the bottle. Make a wish and drop a match in the bottle.

Caution: There is going to be a big flame and the straw and the sword choice are going to be forced out the bottle. KEEP your face and others far from the opening.

In case the straw sticks in the ceiling, then your wish becomes a reality. If the straw does not stick, tell somebody to purchase you a beverage for your hassles. In case you do not get a flame, you need to buy everybody else drinks.

Bar Trick # 12 Blow the Bottle

Ingredients: 1 empty beer bottle, and a little piece of napkin.

Goal: Get a free beverage.

Scenario: Hold an empty beer bottle horizontally. (Make certain interior of the neck is dry.) Detach a little piece of napkin, wad it up into a little ball. Put the napkin wad simply inside the lip of the bottle. Hold the bottle before somebody's face, and wager them a drink that they can not blow the napkin into the bottle.

Answer: Bernoulli principle explains that moving air has lower pressure than still air. For that reason, when your buddy blows, the still air in the bottle is going to press the napkin out of the bottle, right back at the face of the blower.

Keep in mind: The harder they blow, the quicker the napkin is going to come out. In case you get a truly naive person, you can have them attempt once more for a chance at another beverage. You must be able to milk them for at least 3 or 4.

Now, it's time for the responsible part.

Chapter 12: How to Recognize When Enough is Enough

Many individuals believe that alcohol is great. Frequently, in particular dosages, it is. However, there comes a time when you need to tell somebody, "No More." They will not be happy. You will not be popular any longer, however, they'll thank you in the morning.

Well, perhaps the morning after that! However, still, it is essential for you to assist your buddies or patrons to understand that when it's time to stop, it's time to stop. Here are a few dead giveaways:

1. Speech is garbled. When "Another drink please" sounds like "Uhnuva grink peas", it's time to quit.

2. The individual can no longer stand without the help of a prop. To assess this theory, kneel down behind the bar rapidly then come back up. If the customer is on the floor, it's time to stop.

3. When he or she informs you they love you more than two times, it's time to stop. Sure they love you this evening, however, will they value you in the morning?

4. When their bar tab resembles the working annual budget of a little nation, it's time to stop.

5. If anybody begins dancing on the bar-- IT'S TIME TO STOP! Even if it's the hot girl who has actually been flirting with you all night long or the long-retired Chippendale dancer, the show will not be worth the repercussions-- no truly, it will not!

6. If anybody insists they are able to drive, it's time to stop. Sober individuals do not feel the requirement to justify their capabilities to manage a motor vehicle-- drunken individuals do. Cut them off and locate them a buddy to drive them home.

In case you're having a celebration in your home-- with YOU as the bartender, here are some celebration well-being suggestions:

- Do not serve alcohol to somebody under the lawful drinking age. Look at identification; do not enable the serving of alcohol to or intake of alcohol by those without appropriate identification.

- Keep the number of visitors at a workable number; stay clear of violations of tenancy limitations. Do not enable uninvited visitors to "crash" the celebration.

- Do not let visitors blend their own beverages. Select a trustworthy bartender who is going to help monitor the size and number of beverages visitors consume.

- Bear in mind that beer can be just as intoxicating as booze. A 12-ounce can of beer, a five-ounce glass of wine, and a 12-ounce wine cooler consist of the identical quantity of alcohol and the identical intoxication potential as an ounce-and -a-half of liquor.

- Prepare lots of foods so visitors will not drink hungry. Stay away from salted foods, that make individuals thirsty and drink more.

- Keep track of outside activities. Do not enable visitors to bring open containers of alcohol in public locations. Do not enable visitors to park their cars unlawfully.

- Be a great neighbor. Keep music, people-noise and trash/litter levels at a minimum. Clean outdoors litter right away after the celebration.

- Ask energetic or impolite visitors to leave. One such visitor can destroy the celebration for others.

- Offer a range of non-alcoholic drinks for the designated chauffeur and/or for those who choose not to drink.

- Do not push drinks!!! Drinking at a celebration is not obligatory for having fun.

- Close the "bar" 90 minutes before the celebration ends and serve non-alcoholic drinks or foods and coffee. Keep in mind, however, only time sobers who are drunk.

- Politely, yet strongly, inform drunk visitors that you can not let them drive home due to the fact that you care. Arrange for appointed chauffeurs to taxi party-goers to their destination.

- Become knowledgeable about indications of alcohol poisoning and treatment.

- Cooperate with authorities. They are generally there due to the fact that somebody has actually complained. A spirit of cooperation is going to assist in minimizing the requirement for enforcement actions.

For those of you who are considering bartending as an occupation, here are a number of suggestions for you.

Chapter 13: Going to The Big Show

There are bartending schools throughout the nation. An easy Google search is going to reveal you where the closest one to you is. Nevertheless, most neighborhood bars will not care if you have actually gone to Bartending University. On-the-job training is the most effective. However, a fundamental understanding will aid you along the way. I do have a couple of recommendations to assist you along the road.

- Welcome all of your patrons as if you know them and introduce yourself. Remember their names and welcome them, utilizing their names, the following time they drop by. Maintain a legal pad if you need too, "gray beard, thick glasses, name George, drinks Bud" ... and any peculiarities you are able to note that will aid you to remember. Alternatively, you can just state, "Hey, great to see you once again!" Simply think of it like if you were having a celebration in your own house. It's simple!

- Constantly remember what their drink of choice is and be ready to provide them their choice. You ought to already know the names and choices of your regulars.

- If a customer arrives accompanied by a date or buddy, treat them both like they are royalty, address the patron as in "Fantastic to see you once again, Mr. or Ms so and so. (in case they are a regular)" Make sure to utilize the best glass for their buddy. In case you treat them with that kind of regard, you can not just expect a good tip, yet you can wager that they are going to be back repeatedly, and looking for you.

- Your smile and your apparent satisfaction of both your work and your patrons are worth a great deal more than throwing bottles about or performing circus tricks. In case you can do it, well it does not hurt, however a lot of people are there for a beverage, company and the respect and acknowledgment that they do not get in everyday life.

- Depending upon the policy of your company, when customers come in for the initial time, and have simply one beer while reading the newspaper or taking a look around, and after that begin to leave, slide them a complimentary beer/drink and say "I am happy that you came in and I have enjoyed your company," (calling them by name, obviously). "My name is so and so, and please visit us again." Pay for that beer/drink out of your tips in case you must; you are going to get it back, ten-fold.

- Keep in mind that these are customers. They are not truly your friends, so remain professional.

- In case there is problem or violence try, at all costs, to avoid coming out from behind the bar. Raise your voice and try to gain control vocally, while you are calling 911.

- Keep your fellow staff pleased. Their capability to generate income involves how effectively the beverages are made and how rapidly they can provide them, so there is a tender balance in between your bar customers and the table customers.

- Keep an eye on your own customers, and make an effort to prepare for when they may require another beverage. Take care of it, beforehand, and in case you are filling table orders (extremely crucial), constantly acknowledge your bar customers and let them understand that you noticed. Assure them that their beverage is coming right up!

- Even though it is not within your job description, assist the table staff tidy up and turn the chairs. Help them any way you are able to. They are going to want to understand that they have your assistance, so always do what you can to guard their feeling of having an excellent place to work because, despite all your efforts to supply an enjoyable environment for your customers, dissatisfied personnel can diminish that.

- When you have time, hang out talking with your customers. Do not rest on a stool drinking a coke and clearly attempting to find some time alone, even though you are "on break." You can be on break at home. Talk about news, talk about local people and exciting locations, but more notably, make an effort and get them talking about what is essential to them. They aren't in a library, they are in a bar, and perhaps they wish to talk, a lot more than being talked to. It's simple to walk away when you get busy; they can wait and, if they can't, begin determining their intoxication level.

- Thank every patron for having spent their time there with you and, ideally, shake their hand. That kind of thing means a great deal to individuals and will keep them returning. Look them in the eye, especially when they are paying.

- In case that moment isn't available, since you are otherwise included, when you see them rise to leave (and you are confident the bill is cleared), simply holler over your shoulder, "Hey (name), thanks! Take care and get back, OK?"

- Study any bartender's book on blended drinks thoroughly, however, it's just as essential to watch your co-workers blend drinks.

CONCLUSION

Whether you wish to know how to tend bars for enjoyment in your home or professionally as a worker, or perhaps owner of a bar, bear in mind that you are your finest sales representative.

When you understand what you're doing, you are going to be the professional and individuals are going to be coming to YOU for recommendations, beverages, and so much more!

I hope that you enjoyed reading through this book and that you have found it useful. If you want to share your thoughts on this book, you can do so by leaving a review on the Amazon page. Have a great rest of the day.

Made in the USA
San Bernardino, CA
13 November 2019